KONA
LEGENDS

KONA
LEGENDS

by
Eliza D. Maguire

illustrated by
Eva Anderson

Petroglyph Press, Ltd.

Publisher's Note

In this edition, new artwork has been added and the text has been reset, revising the Hawaiian words and place names to reflect currently accepted spelling and punctuation. The references used were the U.H. Press *Reference Map of Hawai'i* by Bier, *Hawaiian Dictionary* by Pukui & Elbert and *Place Names of Hawai'i* by Pukui , Elbert & Mookini. Velda "Maile" Yamanaka also assisted with the spelling of the Hawaiian words. Any suggestions, comments or corrections are welcomed. Enjoy!

COPYRIGHT 1966, 1994, 1999
BY PETROGLYPH PRESS, LTD.
ALL RIGHTS RESERVED.
*This book, or any parts thereof may not be
reproduced without written permission.*

PUBLISHED BY THE PETROGLYPH PRESS, LTD.
160 KAMEHAMEHA AVENUE • HILO, HAWAI'I 96720
808-935-6006 / FAX 808-935-1553
reedbook@interpac.net
www.basicallybooks.com

ISBN 0-912180-54-4

FIRST EDITION
EIGHTEEN PRINTINGS

SECOND EDITION
FIRST PRINTING ~ APRIL 1999
SECOND PRINTING ~ APRIL 2000

Contents

PREFACE

These few legends and stories were told us when Hu'ehu'e Ranch was started in 1886. There were a number of old people living then who showed us these different places with their tales and legends.

I have translated them as they were told, in the simple language of the people living amongst the rural simplicity of life, cultivating their little gardens of *taro* and sweet potatoes, sugar cane and bananas.

When they went to the seashore, they exchanged their products with those of the fishermen, and at the same time exchanged stories real and imaginary, and told legends which had been handed down by word of mouth from their ancestors, generation after generation.

The first we heard was about "'*Akahipu'u*," the hill back of the house. Then we were told of "The Cave of *Mākālei*," where we obtained water from percolations through the roof of the cave. A redwood tank was built in the cave, and water piped to the house. The remains of a piece of '*ōhi'a* wood was found in the cave at that time. It may have been a part of one of the logs which *Mākālei's* father hollowed out into a canoe, and put in the cave, as told in the story of "The Cave of *Makalei*."

We often repeated some of these legends and stories to visitors at the Ranch, but it was not until 1923, when Isaac W. H. Kihe, who was once a Hawaiian school teacher in this section, during the time of monarchy, began writing these tales and legends for "*Ka Hoku O Hawai'i*" (The Star of Hawai'i), a Hawaiian weekly Hilo newspaper edited by Reverend Stephen Desha, that I began to realize that I ought to gather and translate these stories for the future knowledge of our young children who some day may want to know about the history and legends of their own section of country.

So I have translated the legends as well as I knew, taking the best part written by Isaac Kihe, and transposing them within the meaning of what will make fairly good reading, as I lay no claim whatever to any literary ability as a translator. I just tell these legends from the simple language of my maternal tongue into the language of my paternal tongue, if it may thus be designated.

They are simple legends, relating no great deeds of warriors or the *Inoa* (genealogy) of high chiefs. Those belong to historians and men of letters. Mine are tales of *"plain every day folks"*, as we say of ordinary people, and I hope these legends will be found worth reading by *"every day folks"*.

Kekaha (barren, desolate) was the name given to that section of North Kona from *Honokōhau*, north of *Kailua*, to *Nāpu'u* (The Hills) meaning *Pu'uwa'awa'a* and *Pu'uanahulu*, and along the coast to *'Anaeho'omalu*, the boundary of South Kohala. It is often spoken of as *Kekaha-Wai-'Ole* (the desolate land without water). *Pele*, the Volcano, has literally eaten the heart out of this section.

Eliza D. Maguire

Hu'ehu'e Ranch

'AKAHIPU'U

This is a large hill back of *Hu'ehu'e,* and the top of it is sharp and almost pointed. It is the lowest spur of the Mountain *Hualālai,* and that was probably the reason it was called *'Akahipu'u* (The First Hill).

The legend tells how the little *menehune*[a] wanted to take the peak of *'Akahipu'u* off and place it on the top of *Kuili* which is a hill below, near the seacoast.

The hill of *Kuili* has a depression on its top, and the *menehune* thought it would be a fine thing to take the pointed top off *'Akahipu'u* and place it in the hollow top of *Kuili,* for a cap.

'Akahipu'u, The First Hill

These little *menehune* were not only wonderful workers but were often mischievous, and delighted in doing all sorts of tricks.

They started to dig around the top of *'Akahipu'u* and were working away vigorously when suddenly a rooster crowed.

(a) *menehune*~Hawaiian brownies or fairies who were accredited with supernatural powers of accomplishing great things usually in one night.

Down went their *kauila*[b] sticks which they were using as crowbars to pry up the hill top.

The *menehune* stopped working, as it was against their law to work after dawn, but they were most anxious to accomplish this undertaking, for they deemed it a fitting memorial of their great powers as supernatural beings.

They made another attempt again the second night, and again, the rooster crowed.

They were so filled with wrath over the crowing of this rooster, that they decided with one accord to catch and kill him. They sent out three of their number, *Pahulu*, who was their *ali'i* (chief); *Kūhuluko'e*, their marshal, and *Nāhulu*, the messenger.

Moanuiake'a

Now this rooster that crowed so early in the morning and prevented the *menehune* from finishing their work, was also a god. His name was *Moanuiake'a*[c] and he lived in the tall *ohia-lehua* forest about two miles above *'Akahipu'u*.

In the midst of this forest is a beautiful hill with a deep crater filled with ferns and luxuriant vegetation. This hill was also called *Moa Nui a Ke'a*. Below the hill was

(b) *kauila*~A very hard, durable wood used for spears by the ancient Hawaiian warriors.

(c) *Moanuiake'a*~A large chicken that calls; therefore a rooster.

a cave with a pool of water in it, and the rooster lived in the cave.

The water of this cave was *kapu*, forbidden, to women, and this rooster was the guard over this pool of water.

Kāne, who was the greatest god of the forests and the waters, was the possessor of this water and it was he who placed *Moanuiake'a* as its guard.

He also gave him orders to watch the *menehune* digging around *'Akahipu'u* and to prevent them from taking its peak off and placing it on *Kuili*, and thus their plan for distinguishing themselves as most supernatural beings, would fall through.

Let us return and see what *Pāhulu*, the chief of the *menehune*, and his two followers were doing.

They started, as had been arranged, to go and catch this rooster and kill him, so that their work would be accomplished. When *Pāhulu* and his men arrived on the top of *Moa Nui a Ke'a* Hill, they waited until the rooster should crow again. That is also the time when the *'Elepaio* (a Hawaiian bird) sings its *'olēhala*, last note, heralding the dawn, and the *kahuli* (land shell's) piercing song is heard through the woodland.

At last, when these signs of approaching day had died away, the rooster crowed, and these *ākua* (gods) sprang up and caught and killed him.

The third night the *menehune* again started digging around *'Akahipu'u*, while just below them was the *imu*[d] in which they had placed the rooster to *kālua* (bake).

The top of *'Akahipu'u* was about to be raised; the *kauila* sticks were in position, and just as the command was to be given, to *hāpai like* (lift all together), the crow of a rooster was heard from the top of *Moa Nui a Ke'a*.

(d) *imu*~An oven in the ground filled with hot stones, upon which food is cooked.

Menehune digging up the hilltop.

They all stood aghast! Then they began to berate the three *menehune* who had caught and killed the first rooster, and they said: "Why did you not see there was another rooster, and caught and killed him too?"

They argued with one another until at last they uncovered the *imu* and behold! No chicken in the *imu*!

The *menehune* were so enraged at being so fooled, and deprived of their power to fulfill their desire, that they left everything as it was and fled never to appear there again. It was indeed true; the rooster *Moanuiake'a* had come to life again. The god *Kāne* had seen him killed, so he gave him the water of life, and thus he lived again.

After the *menehune* had left *'Akahipu'u, Kaleikini,* a person of power and renown, a distinguished warrior, came and with a *kauila* rod, thrust it nine feet deep, and fastened the hill down firm so that the *menehune* could not come again and take it away.

This *kauila* log was in the side of the hill when we first came to live at *Hu'ehu'e,* but now there is no trace of any *kauila*. A forest of eucalyptus, pine, *kukui* and other trees cover the whole hill.

THE FISH POND OF PĀ'AIEA

This was a very large fishpond extending from *Ka'elehuluhulu*, adjoining the little fishing hamlet of *Mahai'ūla*, and as far as *Wawāloli* on the boundary of *O'oma*.

This pond was not far from *Ka-Lae-O-Keāhole*, (Fisherman's Point) which is the extreme western point, or cape on the Island of *Hawai'i*, and on which there is a lighthouse.

To mariners of the days of sailing crafts, this point was a test of skillful navigation; the wind and tide and current, all combining to thwart the mariner's effort to round the cape, and make the entrance into *Kailua* Bay.

This Fish-Pond of *Pā'aiea* was three miles long, and a mile and a half wide. The fishermen going to *Kailua* and further south, often took a short cut by taking their canoes into the pond and going across, thus saving time and the hard labor of paddling against the *'eka*[a] and also against the strong current from *Keāhole*.

The fishpond of *Pā'aiea*.

(a) *'eka*~A strong sea breeze from the south.

This fishpond belonged to a certain chief, and it was well guarded.

No one was allowed to take or eat a fish without the chief's permission, and from him to the *konohiki* (overseer).

There were houses for the guards and the overseer of the fishpond.

This *konohiki* or overseer's name was *Kepa'alani,* and under him were the stewards and other servants of the chief.

One day an old woman appeared at the large canoe shed of *Kepa'alani.*

The canoes had come in with a large catch of fish,

An old woman appeared asking for fish or *palu*.

aku, (bonito) and the fishermen were cleaning and salting them, and preparing them for drying.

This was the season for *aku*, along the *Kona* coast, and the canoes were filled with fish.

When the people saw this strange woman decorated with a wreath of *ko'oko'olau* [(b)], they greeted her *"Aloha!"* and she returned their greeting, *"Aloha!"*

A man by the name of *Kapulau* said to her: *"Malihini?"* (stranger).

She replied "I am a *kama'āina*,[(c)] not exactly a total stranger, but I do not often come down here to the seashores.

"Living in the restful uplands, and hearing that there was plenty of fish down at the beach, I hastened down to see if the fishermen would give me a bit of *palu*[(d)]."

Kapulau answered: "There is plenty of fish and plenty of *palu*, but we have not the right to give the fish or *palu*; the *konohiki* is the one who has that right. He is sitting over there, and you go and ask him."

The old woman went away, and to the great astonishment of every one, they saw a great crowd of people following her.

When she appeared before *Kepa'alani*, he asked: "A stranger? From where?"

She replied: "From the tangled wilds of the uplands. Hearing of the great quantity of fish down here at the beach I came to get a few."

"No fish," replied the stern overseer.

"The fish is given to the men of the chief. I am only a guardian."

(b) *ko'oko'olau*~A wild shrub with pretty yellow flowers, and dried as a tea.
(c) *kama'āina*~A resident; well known in the place.
(d) *palu*~The intestines of the fish.

"Well! If there is no fish, give me a bit of *palu*."

"There is no *palu*; all given to the men of the chief."

"Then give me a few *'ōpae* (shrimps) from the pond of the chief."

"No! You cannot have fish, *palu*, shrimps or anything. It all belongs to the chief, and only the chief can give them to you.

"Well! That is all. I now return to the uplands without even a grain of salt." The old woman stood up and turned around to go.

When she had gone quite a distance, another great crowd was seen walking around the edge of the pond.

When she came to *Kapulau's* house, she was urged to remain and have something to eat. She consented and sat down. When she had finished her meal, *Kapulau* gave her a fish.

The old woman stood up, and before starting to go, she gave these instructions to her host:

"Tonight, you and your wife put up a *lepa*[e] back of your house, and here on your fence; for it is said, there will be a night of great doings, and tonight may be the night, and you will have your *unuunu* (protection) ready against any evil befalling you."

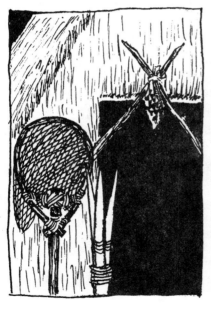

Lepa on the *hale*.

(e) *lepa*~A piece of *kapa* (Hawaiian cloth) tied at the end of a stick as a *kapu* (forbidden) sign.

She turned around and started to go up, but mysteriously disappeared.

Not a sign of anyone to be seen by the people who were watching for her appearance on the plains above.

That night, the people living at the beach, saw a fire on the Mountain of *Hualālai*, and as they saw it coming down its slopes, they realized that the old woman whose request for fish, *palu* and shrimps had been refused, could have been no other than the Goddess *Pele*[f].

The lava came and destroyed the great fishponds of *Pā'aiea*, dried its water and filled and covered it with black rocks.

That is the way the Goddess *Pele* avenged herself on those who did not acknowledge her as supreme, and refused to grant her slightest wish.

(f) *Pele*~The fabled goddess of the volcano.

The Two Girls Roasting Breadfruit

The legend of The Fish Pond of *Pā'aiea*, in the preceeding chapter, tells how an old woman appeared before the fishermen asking for fish, and was told that they would give her nothing, and how, when she left them to go to her home in the mountains, she mysteriously disappeared.

This same old woman soon afterwards appeared at a village called *Manuahi* which was on the western slope of *Hualālai,* and where these two girls who figure in this story, lived.

Two girls roasting breadfruit.

When this remarkable old woman arrived at the village, it was quite deserted and only two girls were there and they were roasting breadfruit.

The name of one of these girls was *Pāhinahina* and the name of the other was *Kolomu'o.*

As soon as the old woman saw them she inquired: "For whom are you roasting your breadfruit?"

The girl named *Kolomu'o* answered: "I am roasting my breadfruit for *La'i.*"

"Who is *La'i?*"

"That is my god."

"Yes? Has *La'i* power?"

"Yes, that is the god of my parents." Then the old

woman turned and asked *Pāhinahina,* the other girl, "and for whom, pray, are you roasting your breadfruit?"

"For *Pele,*" she said.

" Well, if that is so, it is our breadfruit, and it is cooked."

"I do not think it can be cooked, it has only just been turned over."

"Yes, it is cooked, it is smoking."

When they tasted it, sure enough, it was cooked and they ate all of it.

Then the old woman asked her: "Where is your house?"

"Above there, near that hill."

"And where is the house of this other girl?"

"We all live in one house with our parents, she at one end of the house with her parents."

"Where are your parents?"

"Gone to clear land around to plant for the chief."

"When your parents come home, you tell them to put up a *lepa* (sign) on the end of your part of the house."

When her parents came home, *Pāhinahina* told them the instructions this old woman had given her, and they followed it out.

Mysterious instructions of that nature were always followed out, as people of those days believed that only super-natural beings or gods gave instructions in that manner.

That night, after this old woman's visit to the Fish-Pond of *Pā'aiea,* and her interview with the two girls roasting breadfruit, she appeared as none other than *Pele,* the Goddess of the Volcano, who lived at *Kīlauea.*

She evidently was in the habit of traveling about and taking up her abode wherever she fancied, and in 1801 she came over to *Hualālai* Mountain and started her devilish work.

The people, that night, saw a fire on *Hualālai*, at a place called *Ka-Waha-O-Pele*, (The Mouth of Pele) and thought it was the fire of the bird catchers of the *'Ua'u*[a]. Then the fire disappeared, and again lower down, burst forth where the scrub *ohia-lehua* and ferns grew, a place called *Ka-'Iwi-O-Pele*, (The Back-bone of Pele) and it was thought to be a camp fire of the canoe builders.

There the fire flared brightly, then it dwindled down and went out. Soon after, it appeared below *Kīleo*, one of the many spurs of *Hualālai*, and about a quarter of a mile to the right of *'Akahipu'u*, coming out of a little opening and flowing in a thin stream of lava, spreading and growing larger until it covered the south end of the girls' house.

Pele continued her course to the sea and finished her work of destruction.

The cinder hill of *Puhi-A-Pele*, (Pele's Bon-Fire) which looms like a huge castle of ebony, showing in strong relief against the silvery *kukui*[b] grove above it, represents the home of one of the two girls roasting breadfruit which *Pele* destroyed.

It is, at present, a striking landmark plainly visible, about a mile below the road, as one crosses the ridge of the *Kona* mountain.

Pele's Revenge

(a) *'Ua'u*~A species of bird that dives in the sea for fish and takes it to the mountain to eat.

(b) *kukui*~Candle nut tree.

THE POOL OF WAWĀLOLI

This little pool of water is situated near the seashore between *'O'oma* and *Kaloko*. The story of this pool has been handed down from generations past to the present day, and is related thus:

Wāwāloli was the name of a certain *loli* (a sea slug). He was a *kupua* (a wizard). He had two bodies, a limpsy fish body and the body of a man.

There lived in the uplands covered with *'ilima*[a], a man by the name of *Kalua'ōlapa* and his wife, and their beautiful and charming daughter, *Malumaluiki*.

One day she said to her mother that she was going to the beach to gather *limu*, (sea weed), *'opihi*, and *pūpū*[b]. Her mother said she could go.

So she went down, and feeling thirsty, she stopped at the pool to take a drink. She knelt down and, stooping over, drank the cool water.

While she was drinking, she noticed the water began to bubble, and at the same time a shadow was cast over her, and turning around, she saw a handsome young man smiling graciously at her.

"Pardon me," he said, "for intruding upon you in this spot where your beautiful form and face was reflected in the clear depths of this pool."

"Why apologize?" the beautiful girl answered. "We both are strangers to each other, and we meet as strangers at this pool."

The young man again replied, looking at her with adoring eyes, for she was truly very beautiful: "I am no stranger along these shores. I am a *kama'āina*, and

(a) *'ilima*~A shrub whose flowers strung, make the yellow *lei* (wreath) which is now copied with paper.
(b) *'opihi* and *pūpū*~Species of shellfish much relished by Hawaiians.

this is my home, and because I saw you coming down here I came to meet you."

Having thus met they abandoned themselves to the witcheries of love; and the beautiful girl, forgetting her longing for the sea weed and shell fish, for which she came to the seashore, cast her net for more captivating fish. Oblivious of everything, rapt in their own enchantment, time sped on, and the rays of the sinking sun in the western horizon, at last awoke them to the realities of life, and that it was time to part.

Before the girl started on her homeward way, the young man asked her name, and she told him her name was *Malumaluiki*.

"My name," he said, "when we are together is *Wawā*, but my name when you come and sit by the pool you must call *Loli*, and you must call out these words:"

Kaloko Fish Pond

"E Loli nui kīkewekewe
I ka hana ana kīkewekewe
I ku'u piko kīkewekewe
A ka makua kīkewekewe
I hana ai kīkewekewe
E pi'i mai 'oe kīkewekewe
Kā Kāua puni kīkewekewe
Puni Kau'oha kīkewekewe."

TRANSLATION

"O Great Loli, Charmer, Charmer!
Cast thy spell, O Charmer, Charmer,
Of enchantment, Charmer, Charmer,
Over me, O Charmer, Charmer!
Come hither, Charmer, Charmer,
To our tryst, O Charmer, Charmer;
Your heart's desire, Charmer, Charmer,
Awaits you, O Charmer, Charmer."

"O Loli Dear! Behold your heart's desire, your charming one, Malumaluiki, over whom your spell has cast its witching glamour!"

When this compact had been made, the beautiful girl departed, and just at dusk, as the lights were lit in the house, she arrived home.

Her parents inquired: "Why! Where are your 'opihi, limu and a bit of pūpū?

She answered: "That you should ask me when the beach was full of people, and they had gathered everything before I got down there. I could not find a single 'opihi, not a shred of limu, and not even a scrap of anything, so I came home."

As supper was ready, she sat down and ate, and very shortly she arose.

"Finished your supper already?" Said her mother. "I am not hungry; my legs are so tired walking so much today," she said, and went straight to bed, but there was no sleep for her; she tossed and mused and was so consumed with the flames of love, that she could not sleep that night.

At break of day she was up and started again for the beach.

Malumalu'iki calls to *Wāwāloli.*

When she arrived at the pool, she slid into the water, and started to call as she had been taught on the previous day, and immediately this *Loli* appeared in the form of the handsome youth of the day before.

Another day was spent in love making, and so it continued for several days.

In the meantime, the parents of the girl were puzzled over their daughter's actions in wandering to the beach every day and remaining until dusk, and coming home without anything.

So they resolved to spy on her. The next day the father followed his daughter down and saw her reclining on the edge of the pool and heard her call.

"O Great Loli, Charmer, Charmer!
Cast thy spell, O Charmer, Charmer,
Of enchantment, Charmer, Charmer,
Over me, O Charmer, Charmer!
Come hither, Charmer, Charmer,
To our tryst, O Charmer, Charmer;
Your heart's desire, Charmer, Charmer,
Awaits you, O Charmer, Charmer."

"O *Loli* Dear! Behold your heart's desire, your charming one, *Malumaluiki*, over whom your spell has cast its witching glamour!"

The father then saw a *Loli* come out of a hole in the pool and change into a human being. He saw his daughter rapt in the embrace of this being having two bodies, and bestowing caresses upon her with all a lover's ardent fervor, oblivious of everything but their own desires.

The father returned home and told the mother all that he had seen and heard, and when she heard it, she was very sad and at the same time very wroth with her daughter's disgraceful conduct.

Wāwāloli makes love to *Malumaluiki*.

When her husband told her what sort of a lover their daughter had, a double bodied being, a *loli*! She told him to go back and catch this *loli* and beat him to death; and her husband agreed to do so.

The next day he followed his daughter and hid without her seeing him, and he listened intently to the words of his daughter's call, and learned them by heart. After his daughter had started up for home, he went and looked into the pool, and saw a round circle on the water, and he knew there must be a hole below from which that *loli* came up.

He slept that night, and the next day, at dawn he went to the pool with his trapping net and went into the pool giving the call his daughter said, imitating the tone of her voice as nearly as possible.

Malumaluika's father capturing the *Loli*.

As soon as he had finished, the *loli* came out of his hole, and was caught in the ensnaring net and *Kalua'ōlapa* quickly wound the net around so that the *loli* could not escape.

As he was going up, he saw his daughter coming

down, so he hid until she had passed.

When the girl reached the pool she started her usual call. Nothing appeared. She again called and repeated her call until the sun was high in the heavens; not a sign of *loli*, the limpsy fish body, or *Wawā*, the human body.

Thinking him dead she started her wailing, moans, and sobs, calling for her lover in endearing names and bewailing her great loss.

Late in the evening, giving up hope, she returned to her home.

Let us return to where we left *Kalua'ōlapa* with the *loli* in the net. When he arrived home and showed it to his wife she said to him: " Take it to the *kahuna Pāpa'apo'o* who is staying at *Ho'ohila*."

When *Pāpa'apo'o* saw the *loli* in the net and heard the whole story, he told them to prepare an *imu* and bake this "Great *Loli*, Charmer, Charmer."

"When this *loli* is dead, your daughter will live on, and so will all the daughters of the families around here."

They heated the *imu* and cooked the enchanted *loli*.

When the daughter returned home, her eyes were swollen with weeping. Her mother asked her "Why are your eyes so swollen, my daughter?

She did not answer but hung her head.

The father came in and seeing his daughter with her head down, said: "Yes! Your lover with whom you were daily meeting and making clandestine love, is held by the *kahuna, Pāpa'apo'o,* and is now being cooked in the *imu,* so that you and all the other girls with whom this *loli* has been making love, may live!"

This pool is still to be seen with the round hole out of which "the Great *Loli*, Charmer, Charmer," came.

THE CAVE OF MĀKĀLEI

This cave is situated a little above the right of *'Akahipu'u,* the hill back of the home of *Hu'ehu'e* Ranch.

There once lived near this cave a man by the name of *Ko'amokumoku-o-he'eia.*

He came as a stranger from *Ko'olau, 'O'ahu,* and settled here with his wife, whose name was *Kahalu'u,* two daughters and his youngest child, a son named *Mākālei.*

When this man settled in this place, he began to cultivate *taro*[a], sweet potatoes, bananas, sugar cane and *'awa*[b], which all grew without water. The people who

Morning Glory vines over the cave entrance.

had always lived in this part of the country came and told him that the great drawback to this section was no water, except in celebrated caves which are *kapu* (forbidden).

They told him that if he were to get water by stealth from a celebrated cave, and he was found out, he would be killed by the owner of that cave.

When he heard this, he made troughs to catch the water, and when the rains came, he filled his calabashes and troughs.

(a) *kalo* or *taro*~A species of *arum esculentum,* the well known vegetable from which *poi,* the staple food of the Hawaiians, is made.
(b) *'awa*~A plant, the roots of which is made into a stupefying drink.

One day this little boy, *Mākālei*, went to throw some refuse in a sort of hollow, back of the house, and while he was digging around, a cold wind suddenly rushed up, and looking down, he saw a very deep hole.

He was only a little fellow, about three or four years old, and although the wind rushed out and almost took his breath away, he was not frightened, but went to his father who was in his garden and said "I went over there, and while I was digging around a great wind came out of a hole. There must be a wind cave over there."

"Where is it?" Asked his father.

"Down there," said the little boy. His father went to look at what his son had discovered. When *Ko'amokumoku-o-he'eia* arrived at the place his son pointed out to him, he lifted some large slabs of stone which partly closed the hole, and he saw a deep cave extending far in, and a cold wind rushed out as if from the mountain. He turned to his son and said "We have found our own celebrated cave of water in this dry country, and I dedicate it to you. It shall be called *"He Ano O Mākālei."*[c]

"I will fix it so that no one will ever find it." He fixed one side of the entrance of the cave for a rubbish heap, and put a large slab of stone so that the opening of the cave on the other side could not be seen. He told his little son not to tell anyone, not even his mother.

The next day *Ko'amokumoku-o-he'eia* went in by himself. The opening, even to this day, is low, and he crawled in on his hands and knees, and when he got in, he found it a large cave extending far in, for quite a distance. He could stand upright and not touch his head

(c) *He Ano O Mākālei*~Consecrated to *Mākālei*. The word *ana* means cave, but *'ano* literally is the form or appearance of a person or thing. *"He ano"* means to set apart, to consecrate.

to the top of the cave.

Drops of water were dripping from the roof of the cave, and running down the sides

He made up his mind to hollow out canoes of *ohia*[d] and *wiliwili*[e] and fill them with water. He went into this cave at night, carrying in logs of *wiliwili* and hollowed them out, but the *'ōhi'a* logs, he placed in the middle of his garden, hidden by his banana and *'awa* plants.

Mākālei's father carves an *ohia* canoe.

When he had hollowed out the *'ōhi'a* logs, in the shape of canoes, he took them into the cave during the night.

The *wiliwili* logs being light, he hollowed into small troughs, so that he could carry them out filled with water, while the *'ōhi'a* canoes remained as storage containers. He filled the cave with great numbers of canoes, and the interior of the cave was strewn with *wiliwili* troughs and *'ōhi'a* canoes.

When the dry weather came, which often lasts for months in this section of *Kona*, he had nothing to worry about. He went in at night and filled his troughs, calabashes and other containers, and had all the water he

(d) *'Ōhi'a~Metrosideros.* Native forest trees of hard wood from which canoes were hollowed.

(e) *Wiliwili~Erythina.* A soft white wood used for the outriggers of canoes.

wanted for drinking and domestic use. The *kama'āina* were bewildered, and wondered where this stranger got his water from, as there were no signs of water to

Mākālei's father putting a canoe in the cave.

be found around the place.

Some years afterwards, this family moved to *Kaua'i,* and someone else came and lived there, but evidently all traces of the opening of this cave were hidden by the rubbish heap and the *koali* (wild morning glory) vines had grown and twined all over the opening of the cave.

One day there was a great celebration given in honor of some occasion, and all sorts of games and sports were being held. A fine looking young man, a stranger to the crowd, came there and entered into the sports. He seemed to be winning a number of the games. This peeved many of the *kama'āina* youths, especially as the admiration of the women were bestowed on this stranger.

In the intermission between the games, the young man asked for a drink of water. He was told this was a land of no water, especially now, as it was the dry season, and the only water to be found was at the beach where fresh water bubbled out of the sea. The young man said there was water there; the owner of the place denied the assertion, and back and forth they contradicted each other, until the landlord grew very angry, and the crowd cried out to beat and kill this fellow.

Mākālei returns for the games.

He said he would find the water for them; and so it was agreed that if he found the water, the landlord would give one of his beautiful daughters in marriage to him, but if he did not find any water, he would be beaten to death.

He at once went to the rubbish heap, and began to clear it amidst the jeers of the onlookers. A man feeling sorry for the handsome youth laboring so hard to clear all that filth out, set to and helped him. After a while to the great surprise of every one, the mouth of a cave opened out, and following the young man in, they found the floor of the cave strewn with canoes filled with water, clear and cold.

This young man then told them the story of the founding of this cave, and that it was named for him.

"*He Ano O Mākālei*." (Consecrated to *Mākālei*.)

Mākālei married the beautiful maiden, but returned with her to *Kaua'i*.

The cave is known to this day as the *Cave of Mākālei*.

MANINI'ŌWALI

There is a little bay by this name of *Manini'ōwali*[a] situated between *Kūki'o* and *Awake'e*. This bay is like a turquoise gem along this barren lava coast. The water is always a turquoise blue. There is a stone in the form of a woman imbedded in the sand at the edge of the beach, which also bears the name of *Manini'ōwali*. The legend of this stone is as follows:

Manini'ōwali Beach

There were two families living along these lands by the sea, and they were neighbors.

A son was born to one family and he was named *Uluweuweu*, and his home was at *Kūki'o*. A daughter was born, the same day, to the other family, and she was named *Manini'ōwali*, and her home was at *Manini'ōwali* Bay. The parents at their birth declared them betrothed.

They grew to manhood and womanhood. He was fine in form and face, and skilled in the sports of men of those times.

(a) *Manini-O-Wali*~A string of *Manini*. A species of fish, flat in shape and of a greenish gray color with dark vertical stripes.

The girl was very beautiful according to the old Hawaiian type, round and full in form and features.

When the time of the "*hoʻāo*," (announcement of betrothal) was near, great preparations were made for a large feast. The day before the announcement when everything was ready, *Uluweuweu*, the young man, was suddenly taken ill. The celebration was then postponed.

When the young man found that the engagement festivities had been put off, he grew well as quickly as he had fallen ill, and he was seen to *lele kawa* and *heʻe nalu*[b].

Heʻe Nalu

As soon as the folks saw he was well, they began preparations again, for the second time. Again the young man fell ill and nearly died, as they all thought.

For this extraordinary illness of *Uluweuweu*, a *kahuna* whose name was *Kikaua*, was sent for.

When he entered the house, *Uluweuweu* sat up and said to every one around: "Why are you all here? I am not sick."

"Why?" The mother replied. "Because we saw you all doubled up with pain, so we sent for *Kīkaua*, the *kahuna*."

The *kahuna* then said "The boy is not physically ill,

(b) *lele kawa*~To dive off from a high place. *heʻe nalu*~To ride the breakers on a surfboard.

he is, to sum up the whole matter, love sick."

Everyone was speechless with astonishment. Then the *kahuna* said "You all hear what the matter is with the boy. He is in the thrills of first love; the lovelorn looks, sighs and yearnings for the love that reigns within his heart; now burning, now cold as the snow of *Mauna Kea*; the sleepless nights, roaming together with the `Ipo Lei Manu,' (Sweet Love Bird), until the fragrance of dawn is wafted on the zephyrs of the morning.

"Thus it is - a beautiful flower has been disclosed to him; *he mu'o*[(c)] blossoming into the height of perfection.

"That is the spider that has ensnared into her web this bird of the sea-spray and drawn him into the meshes of the net in the mists of the uplands."

When the *kahuna* had finished speaking these riddles, a buzz went around the assembly; questions were asked of each other.

"Who can this person be the *kahuna* is referring to? Who can guess?"

The *kahuna* then said: "It is none other than the brilliant daughter of *Po'opo'omino* and *Ka'eleawa'a*, High Chiefs, and her name is *Kahawaliwali*."

She was a beautiful Princess, and they had been holding clandestine meetings without any suspicion of their tryst, until the *kahuna* brought it out to the knowledge of every one.

Amongst those in the assembly who heard the expose of the *kahuna*, were relatives of the parents of *Manini'ōwali*, and they went and told them all that they had heard from the *kahuna*.

"So the daughter's betrothed is not ill but just in love!"

(c) *he mu'o*~Literally, a bud; figuratively, a growing child, especially of a Chief; in this instance, a young Princess.

"In love with whom?" asked the mother.

"In love with the Princess *Kahawaliwali*; and here we have been thinking he was really ill, but he was only pretending, in order to put off his betrothal ceremonies with *Manini'ōwali.*"

As soon as the mother had heard of this scandal, she immediately went to the parents of the young fellow and told them that the engagement was cancelled and they would have nothing more to do with such a deceitful fellow.

The parents of the boy could not do otherwise than consent to the breaking off of the betrothal.

When *Manini'ōwali* heard all this, and that her betrothal was ended, she became very ill, and *Kīkaua* was sent for.

When the *kahuna* came and saw her, he said: "Well, I thought she was really ill, but no, she is heartbroken; disappointed love!"

The *kahuna* turned to her parents and said: "I have two propositions to place before you. The first is to have the announcement of the betrothal immediately made, without waiting any longer. Second, do away with them all! Which do you choose?"

The mother answered: "Do away with them all!"
"That is the decree!" Said the *kahuna*; and he immediately began to work his black art. He is told as having prayed to his gods, the Goddess *Pele* being the principal one, and the young girls and the young man were all disposed of.

Uluweuweu was turned into a stone which is seen standing at the edge of the sea to this day. He stands on the shore, his lower limbs firm and fast, and where the upper part is joined to the firm rock in the ground, is a groove like a door hinge which rocks back and forth when the waves dash against it.

Kahawaliwali, the Princess, was turned into a long stone about thirty feet high, which stands in the sea. The lower part has two sections, and it is said they represent her legs through which the sea flows continually.

Manini'ōwali, however, was alert and ran and laid down on the sand at the edge of the sea, so when she was turned into a stone she was firm in the sand. When the tide comes in, she is covered, and when the tide goes out the sand is washed away and her form is seen lying clearly outlined on the beach.

But the strangest thing of all is a *ka'awili* (school) of *manini*, in a line so close together that it looks like a string, or a long fish resembling a shark, trails across this little bay of *Manini'ōwali* from end to end.

During the evenings of *Ku*, that is when the moon is in the west at sunset, this string of *manini* is seen; also in the mornings of *Lono* and *Mauli*[d] they follow in a long line. It is said that this *Manini'ōwali* (twist or string of *manini*) is the girl's fish body and she was called that name on that account, and that is why the *manini* strings across this bay named after her.

School of *Manini*.

(d) *Lono*~When the moon is on the wane. *Mauli*~When the moon is on the wane, just before the end.

THE WATERS OF KĀNE

There is a spring of fresh water which bubbles out of the sand along the edge of the sea, on the beach of *Ka'ūpūlehu*. There is a legend connected with the gushing forth of this spring of water. It dates way back to the time when soothsayers, magicians, and the ancient gods had their sway; long before *Pele*, the Goddess of Fire, had come and taken possession of the country from the top of *Hualālai* to the seacoast.

The legend relates that, at that time, there was a chiefess controlling the great division of the land of *Ka'ūpūlehu*, and the adjoining lands of *Kūki'o* and *Manini'ōwali*. She was ruler over thousands of people and the land around was well cultivated.

There came at one time during the reign of the chiefess, a great drought. The sweet potato gardens, the *taro* patches; these principal vegetables which furnished the daily food of the chiefess and her retainers, and her people, were all dried up.

When the last potato and *taro* were gone, they ate the *hapu'u* (the root of the tree fern), the *'ama'u*, (the root of a fern smaller than the tree fern), the *pala*, (the root

Eating *Noni* in hard times.

Page 38

of another variety of fern), the *pia*, (arrowroot), the *hoi*[a] and the *noni*[b].

The sun continued to scorch everything. At last there was nothing to eat. The people grew hollow-eyed and were so weak from hunger that they fell down and slept.

When the chiefess saw the awful condition of her people, she asked her *kahuna*, a priest who had communication with the gods, to intercede for her and her people. "Ask the gods to show us the way to obtain life," she said to him.

The *kahuna* looked on his magic board, and after a while he replied: "O chiefess! The signs show there is no more life, but it is up to you to consider what sins you have committed, that this great affliction should have been put upon you and your people, and to give your consent to the expiation of your faults; and then, only then, can you, your people and your land have life."

The chiefess bowed her head, meditating on what she had just heard from the lips of her *kahuna*.

Raising her head, she asked the priest: "What am I to consent to do for the atonement of my sins in order to gain life for me and my people, and to recover the land from endless destruction?"

The priest replied. "These are the terms imposed upon you. Remain *kapu*[c] and pray for forgiveness during one *anahulu*[d], at the same time implore your brother, *Po'ohuna*[e] in these words:

(a) *hoi*~The bulbous root of a vine eaten in time of scarcity, acrid to the taste.

(b) *noni*~A shrub whose fruit is large and yellow, often used for medicine, not very palatable.

(c) *kapu*~A state of fasting and restriction from intercourse with anyone.

(d) *anahulu*~A period of ten days.

(e) *Po'ohuna*~Literally "hidden head". An appellation of one of the gods-namely, *Kāne* of the Living Waters.

O Kāne, the god of Living Waters!
O Kāne, the Life Giver of our world!
Give unto me and all my people, a great life, a long life, and replenish our land with the life-giving fruits of abundance! "

The chiefess heard these words of her *kahuna,* and she obeyed his instructions, remaining *kapu* for ten days, at the end of which time, having purified herself, she came forth cleansed from all unrighteousness.

The next day a man was seen coming down from the plains above, a stranger to the people.

When he came into the presence of the chiefess, she recognized him as her godly brother to whom she had been praying for aid, *Kāne* of the Living Waters. She sprang up and kissed her brother.

The chiefess purifies herself.

Kāne asked: "What is all this trouble over the land and the people of the chiefess?"

"What indeed, but a terrible affliction has befallen upon us and all the country around! The sun has dried up all living plants, the earth is so parched nothing will grow, we have no food, no water, we are all faint and dizzy and cannot walk and are lying down nigh unto death."

"You are indeed in great *pilikia* (trouble)," said *Kāne*. "I knew you must be in trouble, because these signs which I feel always foretell trouble, and they urge me to go forth and locate them. The hair on my head began to *'e'eu* (creep) and *ka loku o ka poli o ku'u wawae* (the arch of my feet ached) so I knew you were in trouble and needed me and I came to find out."

Kāne called all the men who were able to walk to go and get plenty of firewood. There were about a thousand or more who went for firewood.

(*He mau lau*). *Lau* is four hundred; *mau* means more than two, so there must have been a thousand or more who had strength to go. We must remember that *Kāne* was the great life giving god, and probably gave these men strength to gather firewood.

When the men returned with a great pile of firewood *Kāne* told them to make an *imu*. The men did as they were instructed. When the *imu* was intensely hot, *Kāne* told them to bring *'ākulikuli*[f] and *makaloa*[g] and great quantities of these things were brought.

Kāne then said: "*Ulu ka imu.*"[h].

But what seemed strange, no food was seen put into the *imu* after the embers and ashes were thrown out.

Kāne still directed them: "Put on the *'ākulikuli* and the *makaloa*; spread them thick."

When spread, *Kāne* laid down on the *imu* and told them, "Put on dirt and *makaloa* until I am covered out of sight."

The men put on the dirt and *makaloa*; and the more they put on the higher grew the *imu*, until at last they gave up trying to cover it.

(f) *'ākulikuli*~A kind of water herb.
(g) *makaloa*~A kind of rush from which very fine mats are made.
(h) "*Ulu ka imu*"~Throw out the embers and ashes, ready for putting in food to cook.

While the men were shouting over this man being buried in the *imu*, *Kāne* appeared from below and demanded the *imu* to be uncovered, and the strange *imu* was immediately uncovered. When it was laid bare there was heaped up food all cooked.

One side had *taro*, another potatoes, breadfruits, yam, arrowroot; and all these things were ready, and the people sat down and ate; and what was left over, the *kahuna* divided it all around.

When *Kāne* laid down on the *imu* he appeared in the sea, and the opening where he came forth again was a bubbling spring, and it was called *"The Waters of Kāne"*.

On account of *Kāne* being *pulehu* (roasted) in the *imu*, this beach is called *Ka'ūpūlehu*[i], and not only the beach but the great division of land from the mountain to the sea.

Kāne, the *imu* and the bubbling spring.

(i) *Ka'ūpūlehu*~Literally, *Ka-imu-pulehu A-Ke-Akua.* The oven in which the god was roasted.

THE CATCH OF THE GODS

In olden days, at the fishing hamlet of *Makalawena*, the story is told of mysterious fishing with supernatural beings.

The fishermen casting their net at night would think that those alongside of them were their own fellow companions. The net would be dragged down with the weight of the fish, but as soon as the net was hauled ashore, not a single fish would be in it. The fishermen would sometimes dive down when the net felt heavy, but the sea would flash and flame like forks of lightning[a] and dazzle their eyes, so that they could see nothing.

Net Fishing from shore.

This happened so frequently that the fishermen were exasperated, and held council to decide on a plan for exterminating these devilish *akua*.

They decided to get *Puniaiki* of *Kohala*, for he was renowned as a destroyer of *akua;* he knew how to catch them.

A messenger was sent to *Kohala*. When he arrived in *Kohala*, he made inquiries as to where *Puniaiki* was to be found. He was shown the way to his house, and on meeting

[a] This probably was due to the phosphorescence, but the legend relates it as the work of the *Akua*-devils.

Puniaiki, he related to him the object of his visit.

Puniaiki said to him: "Tomorrow we start, as this day is over, and we must not travel at night; in the meantime we will weave a net to catch the gods.

Puniaiki weaves an enchanted net.

"The messenger replied: "Why waste time making a net? My house is filled with nets of every description."

"Maybe nets only in quantity, but not the quality that would catch *akua* or devils; for how is it you have not been able to catch them", said *Puniaiki*.

They wove a net of the very finest mesh, and when finished they put it in a *hōkeo*[(b)] so that the *akua* could not see it.

Early the next morning they started, following the seacoasts till they came to a place called *Kaiʻōpae*, and found a canoe going to *Kekaha*, North Kona, to fish for *ʻahi* (albacore) and they got on as far as *Makalawena*, and went ashore.

(b) *Hōkeo*~A long gourd or calabash used by the Hawaiian fishermen for carrying fishing tackle.

When they landed, *Puniaiki* told his companion not to tell anyone a single thing about him, or about his journey to *Kohala*, not even to call his name, *Puniaiki*, but to call him *Kalepeāmoa*, cock's-comb, on account of his bald head.

Puniaiki, or *Kalepeāmoa* as we shall now call him, began getting acquainted with the people. He told his friend to prepare the nets, and instruct certain ones to take turns as *kāpeku*[(c)]. There were to be two shifts of splashers.

The night shift would be those who were to begin with him in the early part of the night, and the day shift at the finish.

The splashers were all to sleep during the day. Then at night, one set was to start with him, but they were to splash the water only on the edge; he alone was to swim out with the fine meshed net.

When he gave one whistle then one splasher was to dive and swim out to him; when he whistled again two were to swim out, whistled again, three, and so on until all the splashers of the night shift were out; then all the splashers of the day shift were to join in pulling in the net.

The splashers were all ready, and *Kalepeāmoa* walked out, while he saw the *akua*, little devils, watching him.

Then he swam out beyond his depth and whistled. Instantly one of these devils jumped into the fine meshed net, and *Puniaiki* rolled and strangled him to death.

He whistled again; another little devil jumped in and was finished in the same manner, and so on until

(c) *Kāpeku*~Splashers. Those who splash the water to drive the fish into the net.

five *kāuna*[(d)] were caught. Then *Puniaiki* called to the splashers whom he had left for the last, to come out with their net and they all swam out and let the net down and dragged in this big catch of the gods.

The fishermen had no more trouble in filling their nets with fish, as they were rid of the little devils.

The place has ever since been called *Ku'una-A-Ke-Akua*, The Catch of the Gods.

Sailing on a *Kona* bound fishing canoe.

(d) *kāuna*~ A group of 4, so 5 *kāuna* would be 20.

THE HILL OF MOEMOE

Moemoe was the name of a prophet who was under the command of the Goddess *Pele*. The legend relates how this prophet, *Moemoe*, saved the population of *Nāpu'u* (The Hills), meaning *Pu'uanahulu*, and *Pu'uwa'awa'a*, from being devoured by a Shark-God who inhabited that part of the country. He was also a *kūkini makanipuahiohioi* (a whirlwind runner). The hill of *Moemoe* was named after him, and there was a saying about the hill of *Moemoe* with reference to the person *Moemoe*.

"Brush of *Moemoe*, brush of *Moemoe*. Where is *Moemoe*?" The brush of *Moemoe* answers:

"Gone long ago; only the day is left to me."

Moemoe was so swift, he was gone long before the rays of the sun could touch him or the flat hill of *Moemoe*. When *Moemoe*, the prophet, arrived at this hill, and sat down to rest, he heard the sound of voices loudly talking as they were rushing down to the beach. He turned around and saw a great crowd of people talking excitedly, so he went to see what it was all about.

When he arrived there, a great crowd was gathered around, and he beheld a game of *kōnane*[a] being played on the *papa kōnane* of the Chief *Ka'uali'i* and the Chiefess *Welewele*. When he came nearer, he found one of the players was a man from the uplands of *Nāpu'u*, whose name was *Iwahaonou*[b], and he recognized him as a two bodied being, a human body and a shark body. The people did not suspect this *Iwahaonou* as anything else than a man, but *Moemoe* recognized him right away

(a) *kōnane*~Hawaiian checkers played on a stone checker-board (*papakōnane*) with shells.

(b) *iwahaonou*~Literally, stuffed mouth. A mouthful.

as a *aīwaīwa*[(c)], sitting there as a human being, but capable of turning into a shark, and devouring all these people around him.

As soon as *Moemoe* sat down, *Iwahaonou* began immediately to quiz him.

"Say! Do you know the *no'a*[(d)], if not, perhaps the *kōnane?*"

Moemoe answered: "I have learned all those games; also the *kūkini*, the *kilokilo'ōuli*[(e)]; to prophesy the weather, storms and calm; to predict the future, life or death; to know the appearance of a man, woman, child, old man and bent and crippled old woman."

"Yes! You do know a great deal! You can fathom from childhood to old age when the eyes are dim, the steps totter, and the breath is short! Indeed! And pray, who are you and what is your name?"

Moemoe plays *kōnane* with *Iwahaonou*, the man-shark.

(c) *aīwaīwa*~A fabulous person.
(d) *no'a*~A game of hiding a stone called *no'a* and guessing where to find it.
(e) *kilokilo*~Prophesying (*ouli*-omens); predicting omens.

"I am not going to tell you my name, until you tell me yours first, for that was not your first question; the *no'a* and the *kōnane* was what you wanted to match your skill with mine; and let me tell you, I can just knock this coward of a braggart clean over the *pūkolu*[f] like the wind of *lau niu*; you hear me."

Iwahaonou tried to pass it off, but not so the assembly. With one accord they shouted in favor of *Moemoe* to *kōnane*.

When *Iwahaonou* saw that the crowd favored the *malihini* (stranger) he said: "I am going to ask you, nameless stranger, to let us first go and have a sea-bath, then, when we come back, we will feel refreshed, ready to compare our skill."

Moemoe replied: "You had better go and bathe yourself. The dirt is so thick on you that it is caked, as if you had always slept in the dirt, and just came down here to shake the dust and spread it like a cloud of smoke rising high and overshadowing our backs."

Iwahaonou was filled with anger, because he was told that he was so dirty, the dirt had caked on him.

He stood up and said: "You wait here for me, and when I return, we will have our sport, but if I return and you are gone, I will follow till I find you and I will crush *poi* for bait to catch sharks with."

"I shall be delighted also to meet you and test our skill and strength, and you will see how I will bend you like the twigs on the tree, not one twig that a bird can rest on, green or dry, will be left, and that is how I will bend your bones," *Moemoe* answered.

After *Iwahaonou* had left, the assembly began discussing the affair of *Moemoe* and *Iwahaonou*.

Then *Moemoe* asked the people "Are you well acquainted with this man?"

(f) *pūkolu*~The name of a triple canoe; three canoes rigged abreast.

They said "Yes, we all know him. He lives up *Nāpu'u* and he often comes to bathe in the sea."

Moemoe told them that this was not a human being He had a shark body and a shark mouth on his back, that is why he wore the *pa'ūpa'ū*[g] cloak to hide his back.

"That is the shark that is eating all these people who go down to the beach to bathe or fish.

When he sees them going down, he then comes along and engages them in conversation."

"You are going to the seashores?"

"Yes, we are going for a sea-bath."

"Yes, the shark hasn't had his breakfast yet."

"That man with the shark body who has gone down, is not really going sea-bathing. He has gone to eat those people who have gone fishing for *opihi*, crabs and to dive for *wana* (sea eggs).

"We will hear the sad news, today, that those people have all been eaten up by the shark. The country will be depopulated, if you do not kill this man-shark. If you do not believe me, prove it yourselves by catching this man. Take good care he does not get away, and also be careful how you grab him in the back, or his great shark mouth will bite off your hands."

Moemoe told them to build an unusually large *imu*, When it was ready, and the man-shark had been cooked, they must be very careful how they threw out the pieces of unburned wood, and see that the ashes or anything from the *imu* did not get wet with the salt water, for if it did, this man-shark will come to life again.

Let us learn a little more about *Iwahaonou*, the man-shark. He lived at a place called *Puaka-hale* at *Pu'uana-hulu*, the latter a hill not unlike Diamond Head in outline.

(g) *pa'ūpa'ū*~Old, worn out *tapa* (cloth), filthy, dirty.

He lived there, and planted sweet potatoes, *taro*, sugar cane and bananas, and the road to the beach was alongside of his home.

As the people passed by, he would call out: "You are going to the beach?".

They would answer "Yes."

"The shark hasn't had his breakfast yet! Do not take any sugarcane named *Hui*, for that sugarcane is *kapu*, belonging to *Hui*, the Shark-God of this coast."

Iwahaonou in his shark form.

The people paid no attention, but continued on their way to the beach. When part way down below the *pali* (precipice) *Kapa'ala,* and lower down near the cave of *Nā'alu,* they would hear these words being called after them.

"They are carrying the *Hui* sugarcanes."

Then they would throw the cane away, and a great stack would be found along the road near this cave of *Nā'alu.*

Now this *Iwahaonou*, talking to these people and explaining about the sugarcane of *Hui*, was *Hui* himself, the Shark-God. When the people had gone on to the beach he would rush down, arrive there first, pretend to be watching the chiefs playing *kōnane*, and chuckle to himself over his cunning ruse. This had happened several times, and quite a number of people had been eaten by the shark, never suspecting this man was a man-eating shark. Terror reigned all over the land.

Let us return to the people who had followed *Moemoe's* instructions in preparing the huge *imu*, ready to cook *Iwahaonou*, and were waiting for him.

In the meantime, they heard screams and wailings of the men, women and children being devoured by the shark.

As soon as *Iwahaonou* appeared before *Moemoe* and the people who were waiting for him, at a nod from *Moemoe* the men jumped and caught him. As he was struggling another lot came, helped hold him down and tied his feet and hands. When they took off his old dirty cloak sure enough, there on his back was the huge mouth of the shark wide open, his sharp teeth showing, and his eyes ablaze like balls of fire rolling from side to side.

While he was lying there, *Moemoe* summoned all those men whose wives and children had just been eaten by this man-shark, to throw him into the *imu*. Almost immediately after he had been thrown into the red hot *imu*, he was cooked to a crust and crumbled into a heap of ashes.

That was the end of the man-shark and the people were safe to fish and bathe in the sea thereafter.

This land of *Nāpu'u* was and is now a very large division of land, and was well populated in ages past, it was largely cultivated for the *Ali'i Keawe-Nui-a-Umi* (Great King *Keawe*, son of *Umi*). *'Ehu* was appointed chief of this division, and for the reason of *'Ehu* peacefully governing here, the saying has been celebrated in songs descriptive of *Kona* which have been handed down to the present day as *"Kona I ka La'i a 'Ehu,"* (*Kona* in the Calm of *Ehu*) also *"Kona Kaimalino a 'Ehu,"* (*Kona* of the Smooth Sea of *'Ehu*).

The people were safe to return to the sea.

THE POND OF WAINĀNĀLI'I

Wainānāli'i (The Water Belonging to the Chiefs) was considered the largest and most celebrated fishpond on the Island of *Hawai'i*, in fact, the largest in the whole group said to contain an area of 600 acres or more. It was situated near *Kīholo*. On a map published in the Paradise of the Pacific magazine, May, 1925, *Wainanarii*[a] is written on the western coast of *Owyhee*, as the Island of *Hawai'i* was then called. The map was published, according to the Paradise of the Pacific, London, November 7, 1843, by John Arrowsmith.

So it shows, this pond must have been of some note before the great flow of 1859 destroyed it. The great lava flow of 1859, not only filled and destroyed this pond, but formed a lava promontory extending out into the ocean.

A legend is told of two young girls who were stationed as guards over this great fishpond.

They were *kupua*, wizards, and had two forms, a human and a lizard one. They were often seen in their lizard form sunning themselves on the stone wall of the pond.

One day these two girls were in their human form, and had just returned from a swim in the sea. They were drying their flowing tresses when the Goddess *Pele* had come down the slope of *Mauna Loa,* and had crossed over. She was racing down from *Pu'uanahulu* to destroy the Fish-Pond of *Wainānāli'i*. She seems to have had a mania for destroying fishponds. *Pele* spied these two beautiful girls, and before they could move, she covered them with her mantle of lava.

(a) *wainanarii*~The foreigners who first came to the Islands, always spelled words, using r for l; t for k, and b and d, which are not in the Hawaiian alphabet.

Kanikū (*kū* means standing) and *Kanimoe* (*moe* means lying down or sleeping) are now two lava slabs, side by side, and as their names indicate, one erect and the other flat, just as *Pele* had caught them.

These two lava slabs are on the old trail across the lava flow of 1859. Twenty-five and thirty years ago, this rough trail was the only road one travelled along the coast between *Kona* and South *Kohala*. The trail was marked with the bones of animals who had fallen on the way, and also with white coral stones.

In sections of this trail, on ancient lava flows, are markings, (petroglyphs) representing ancient Hawaiian myths and history.

Pele seems to have respected these marks of history. They may have represented some eulogy in her favor and so spared them. No one will ever know, though, how many she may have ruthlessly covered.

Petroglyph Field

Books by the PETROGLYPH PRESS